MILA BOUTAN

Renoir and me

A & C Black • London

If I said RENOIR to you, what would you say?

Renoir

OH RENOIR!

I recognise his paintings immediately.

The colors are bright and warm, and it is summer.
People are dancing, and everything is beautiful,
full of happiness and music.

The children are happy.
You can almost hear them laughing.

Pierre Auguste Renoir was born in 1841.

His father was a tailor in Paris.
Renoir originally trained to paint porcelain
– beautiful china plates and cups.
He was very good at this,
but he grew bored of it,
and dreamt of being a real painter.
He took some painting classes in a studio,
where he met a group of young artists
who were looking for a new way of painting.

They wanted to paint what they saw —

Outdoor landscapes and the impressions
everyday life made on them.
Things were made easier for them
because chemists had invented tubes of paint by then
so that they could work outside.

The Impressionists

Renoir, Claude Monet and Alfred Sisley, amongst others,
invented modern painting;
they were later known as 'the Impressionists'.

Renoir and Monet
had been friends for a long time.
Look at the sailing boats they painted together!
Although the paintings look similar,
we can see the difference in the way each artist
sees and expresses himself, how they paint
with different marks and colors.

Renoir was independent,
making his own way. He also found a patron
to support him.
He could see that Renoir had a touch of genius!
Renoir became a success.
But he still wanted to learn how to
draw and paint better,
so he travelled to Italy,
to look at paintings by the old Italian Masters.

Influenced by these great painters, the
paintings of Renoir's last thirty years
became simpler, more natural,
filled with color and life.

Madame Charpentier

A large, quiet room, a sleeping dog, an elegant woman
sitting on a sofa, two well-behaved children.
On a side table is a beautiful bouquet of flowers. There is a soft rug,
a background of wallpaper and curtains; everything is in harmony.

There is nothing very surprising about this: there were hundreds of
portraits like this at that time, but Renoir is original in the
way he gives as much importance to the two children with
their blue dresses as he does to their mother.

As for the woman, it is her black dress we notice rather than her face.
The décor, which surrounds the people, is suggested by the colors,
not painted in detail.

A Triumph!

Madame Charpentier, the wife of the editor who published **Emile Zola**, and strong supporter of writers and artists, 'launches' Renoir. He becomes a **fashionable painter** and people commission him to paint for them.

But what does **Renoir** do?
He goes to Italy to see the work of the Great Masters.

Dancing
They dance, celebrate, enjoy themselves and are happy!

Renoir enjoyed himself as well and wanted to share this joy.

In these pictures, look at the young woman's face
turning away as the young man tries to kiss her!
However, the red and yellow hats blend into
each other, almost as if they want to embrace.
Can you see the yellow hat which is rolling on the ground
and the fan, both giving the impression of **movement?**

Have you noticed the billowing dresses that **Renoir**
has used so well to suggest **dancing?**
And the dinner jacket and the dancer's white gloves?

If I ask you: who is the main subject in the painting?
The woman in the light dress? Or the man in the dark suit?
You would probably answer the woman in the **light** dress.
But it is the man's **dark** suit which brings out
the dancer's **beauty** and **joy.**

Do Pablo Picasso's couple
with their **straight** arms, express the same feeling
of pleasure?
Do they want to dance and look at each other?
What about the colors?
And the woman's hat........?

Picasso, also with the skill of a genius,
paints **a less happy** vision
and makes you feel a completely different emotion.

If Renoir paints a scene of love,
Picasso paints a scene of **lovelessness**.

What an enormous difference
between the two painters!

What would you say about this?

Children

Gabrielle, a cousin from the country, came to live with **Renoir** and his family to look after his children and then later the sick painter himself. She stayed 20 years with them and became the **painter's** favorite model, thanks to her **cheerfulness, down-to-earth** character and her natural, everyday **gestures.**

Here she is with a **baby, Jean,** the future film director.
Look how **Jean's** arm follows **Gabrielle's,**
showing the affection this young girl has for the little boy.
You will find her in a lot of Renoir's masterpieces.

Renoir **adored children** and often painted his three sons:
Pierre, Jean and Claude.

You see this beautiful little girl,
her long golden hair tied with a pretty pink ribbon?
In fact it's not a girl,
it is Claude, nicknamed Coco, one of Renoir's sons!

This **baby** with a **bonnet** on his **head**
is **Coco** again,
dressed in a little girl's **dress**,
quite normal for baby **boys** at that time.

He is dressed all in **white**, looking almost like a **meringue**, on a
green background, with his **spoon** in his hand.
Maybe he is waiting for his supper!

This one is Jean. He is wearing a Pierrot Clown costume, all white,
and much too big for him.

He looks like he is losing his balance.

Do you notice how all the folds help this mass of white to come alive?

What do you think?

His little face, with a pointed hat on top, looks like it has been placed
on top of the bright red ruffed collar.

Claude again, dressed in a funny-looking red silk romper suit with a lace collar.
What do you think about this?

Can you imagine posing, without moving, dressed in a costume like this?
What about the white tights? Claude didn't want to put them on,
but Renoir insisted, as the white makes the other colors shine out.
Thirty years later, Jean remembered an argument between his
brother and father....because the tights were itchy!

Like **Renoir**, Picasso did a portrait of his son Paul
dressed in a Pierrot costume.
Can you see the differences between the three works?

What do think about the backgrounds of Picasso and Renoir's paintings?
Floor, wall and balcony: Picasso places his son Paul, in white,
in front of three bold-colored rectangles. Renoir places
Claude, dressed in red, against a harmonious background,
with the ruff and tights bringing the red to life.
The column on the wall in the background balances the painting.
Renoir paints his son looking slightly hesitant,
but Picasso's son looks much more sure of himself.
Two ways of seeing the same subject..........

Here, it is Jean who is drawing, with his nose almost touching
the paper and his elbows spread out on the table.
He doesn't look posed in this one!
Compare the way colors are used in these portraits.
You can see that Renoir has used white again to highlight the face.
Notice also how the hands express the child's concentration.
Do you feel **Renoir**'s fatherly tenderness?

Jean became famous by making films, where he brought the
atmosphere of his father's paintings alive on screen.
He also wrote a beautiful book of memories dedicated to Renoir.

Renoir enjoyed painting his son Jean in modern hunting clothes in the same pose that **Diego Velázquez** had chosen for the Spanish child painted three centuries earlier.

Renoir
knew the great painters and was not afraid of comparisons.....

Let your imagination go as you look at this painting....
Two young girls very close to each other. One is reading out loud,
the other, her head resting on the palm of her hand,
listens with pleasure.

Renoir has chosen to fill the whole canvas with these models
and to paint the two faces in the shadow of their hats,
making it look like there is only one of them.
Can you see what Renoir was trying to do? He wanted to express
the intimacy and tenderness of the two young girls.
Their hats are the most moving element in the painting.
You would like to know what they are reading with so much pleasure.
But we cannot see the title....it is a mystery.

This painting shows two young girls
reading in broad daylight.
What a difference from the one before!!!
The colors are almost washed out,
the arms are hardly noticeable, the
characters' expressions are uncertain.
One could say Renoir was getting a bit bored!
Do you think he did it just for the pleasure
of having fun with the hats?
Jean says that his father adored painting hats.

Not AGAIN!

You say each time you see a new
painting! But this one, painted in
blue tones, is of a mother with grey
hair and a dark dress sitting in
profile and her daughter, facing us
with a large hat and loose hair. The
mother, Berthe Morisot, was a close
friend of Renoir's, the sister-in-law
of Edouard Manet, and a painter
herself.

In an apartment of that period,
you see two sisters at a piano, reading a music score.
The brunette is standing up, listening and leaning over the blonde
girl in order to read the notes better.
With the hand movements,
Renoir has created a space in the middle of the painting,
which emphasises the two faces.
Renoir's aim is to express **without words** a feeling of unity,
a shared emotion, between the two young girls,
Does he succeed? What do you think?

Gabrielle

In these portraits of a woman, you recognise straight away
Gabrielle with her beautiful face, round cheeks, small nose
and red lips. It is this type of fresh beauty, like a ripe fruit,
that Renoir liked and painted up to the end of his life.

Wearing very simple clothing, silent, ignoring the painter's
presence, absorbed by her sewing, reading and brushing her hair,
Gabrielle is always **concentrated** on what she is doing.
You notice that they are scenes painted indoors, each one creating
a different impression.

Gabrielle, with her round face, is the same young woman,
but, this time, is dressed in a shiny, transparent fabric,
open at the bust, with a flower in her hair.
She is dreaming, her head tilted, a necklace around her neck
as she holds another rose in her hand.

See how the painter has chosen different colors,
using dark red in this painting, whilst he exaggerates
the contrast between light and shadow.
This is another kind of beauty, which Renoir tries to express.

Landscapes

Like all the painters of this era, Renoir painted outside.
He liked the light of the Côte-d'Azur where he had a house built
when he could no longer walk.
Here, there is a vineyard framed by two olive trees,
and in the distance a bluish-colored mountain.
Nothing is drawn, apart from the forked trunks of the two trees.
Everything else is expressed by the touches of light placed on
the areas of green and red.
Look how the character in the foreground is painted
just with some brush marks.

In this painting all the charm comes from the transparency created by the curtain of trees which allows one to perceive a house in the background.

Below is the village of Cagnes, where Renoir spent the last years of his life. The landscape is very composed, with the houses climbing towards the sky.

Can you see the woman resting between the palm trees?
Compare her with the one you can see in the shade of the olive tree.
Can you see how the vegetation has changed?

Lifelong friends Paul Cézanne and Renoir painted the Sainte-Victoire mountain near Aix-en-Provence together.

Cézanne's painting shows the mountain as a huge and almost menacing rock. Renoir, however, seems to want to soften the mountain, paying more attention to the shadows of the trees in the foreground and the yellow sky.

An admirer of Renoir, Pierre Bonnard, shows us a very different vision of a garden in bloom – it's a firework display of pure colors in vertical and diagonal lines.

The painting creates a feeling of freshness, and it is overflowing with light at the same time. Look at the wonderful variety of tones: reds, violets, mauves, pinks, greens and yellows…..

The Bathers

Like many other painters before him, Renoir shows us
the beauty of the body, running water, light and nature,
all in one go.

The bathers are surrounded by thick vegetation, which is hardly
drawn. We have the impression that their bodies are part of nature,
like the flowers and grasses in the background. Renoir expresses
himself better in a painting than he does with words and conversation.

These nude young women in the water, under the leaves of the trees, are illuminated by a light which glistens on their hair and arms. Can you see how youthful and full of life they look? They look destined to stay like this, thanks to the wonderful water and light.

You will understand Renoir's bathers better if you compare them with **Picasso's**. He has removed the background vegetation and replaced it with cold colors and shapes.
He exaggerates the differences of light and shade. The feeling of people being in harmony with nature has disappeared!

Don't these people look almost like statues, made of wood or marble?
Renoir's bathers are very much alive, though. They are breathing the scent of the leaves and listening to the birds singing!
Full of life, they feel as if they are about to rise up and enter the water.

The Washerwomen

What is this painting telling you?
It is about women on the riverbank who are washing their
clothes under the trees, with the sea in the background.

Renoir wanted to tell a story, like a cartoon. These women,
out in the fresh air, are carrying their washing in large
baskets on their heads.
They wash, scrub, rinse and wring, then put the washing to
dry on the grass in the sunshine.
Happily at work, they are in harmony with the landscape around
them. Renoir has painted them as soft silhouettes which seem
to melt into the vegetation.

It seems that Gabrielle posed twice for this painting of two washerwomen. Renoir has used the same style, but the image is clearer and more precise, showing the strength in Gabrielle's arms – but she is also graceful. He obviously enjoyed painting these pictures.

These are the habitual colors used in Renoir's paintings, this red and the areas of white, which highlight the whole painting. Look at the brush marks: the small dots look like flower petals, the leaning lines show grass and the wavy brush marks suggest ripples in the water.
For clothes, Renoir uses softer brushstrokes.

The Patrons

Renoir was lucky to have been supported all his life by important patrons who were sure that he had a wonderful talent.
This is a portrait of Paul Durand-Ruel who was the first one to discover his friend's talent and who introduced him to the great collectors.

This gentleman, disguised in a bullfighter's costume, is Ambroise Vollard, who greatly admired Renoir. Why did Renoir do this portrait of him as a bull-fighter in red and green, with pearls and pink tights? Strange for a patron! Without doubt, the artist wanted to produce a brilliant painting for this friend, but Vollard looks more like a patron than a bull-fighter, thanks to his rather serious and thoughtful expression.

Self-portrait

This old man with a small beard and hat is Renoir – the painter of **joy**. He has painted children, young women and flowers,

thousands of paintings – six thousand, he said – which have been spread throughout the world into museums and private collections. They are, however, the work of just one man, who died almost 100 years ago, in 1919. He has been universally admired, for the way he painted beautiful, happy and interesting pictures right up to the last day of his life.

Throughout your life,
his work will remain an image of **joy** for you.

Piero della Francesca
1422-1492
Detail of a fresco "*Legend of the True Cross*"

Renoir

always spent a lot of time in museums.

In Italy, he went to see the works of Raphael, Titian and Piero della Francesca.

"I didn't know how to paint nor draw."

"It is by looking at a painting that one decides to become a painter."

Rubens
1577-1640
Portrait of
Isabelle Brandt,
Ruben's wife.

"When I look at the Old Masters, I feel like a very small man."

Self-portrait of Raphael.

Raphael
1483-1520
Portrait of Balthazar Castiglione

When he saw the *Seated Virgin* by Raphael Renoir said:

"It is the freest, simplest and most vivacious a painting can be."

In Madrid, at the Prado, he admired Velázquez the painter and above all the pink ribbon of the infant

Margarita.

"All the art of painting is in this one," he said.

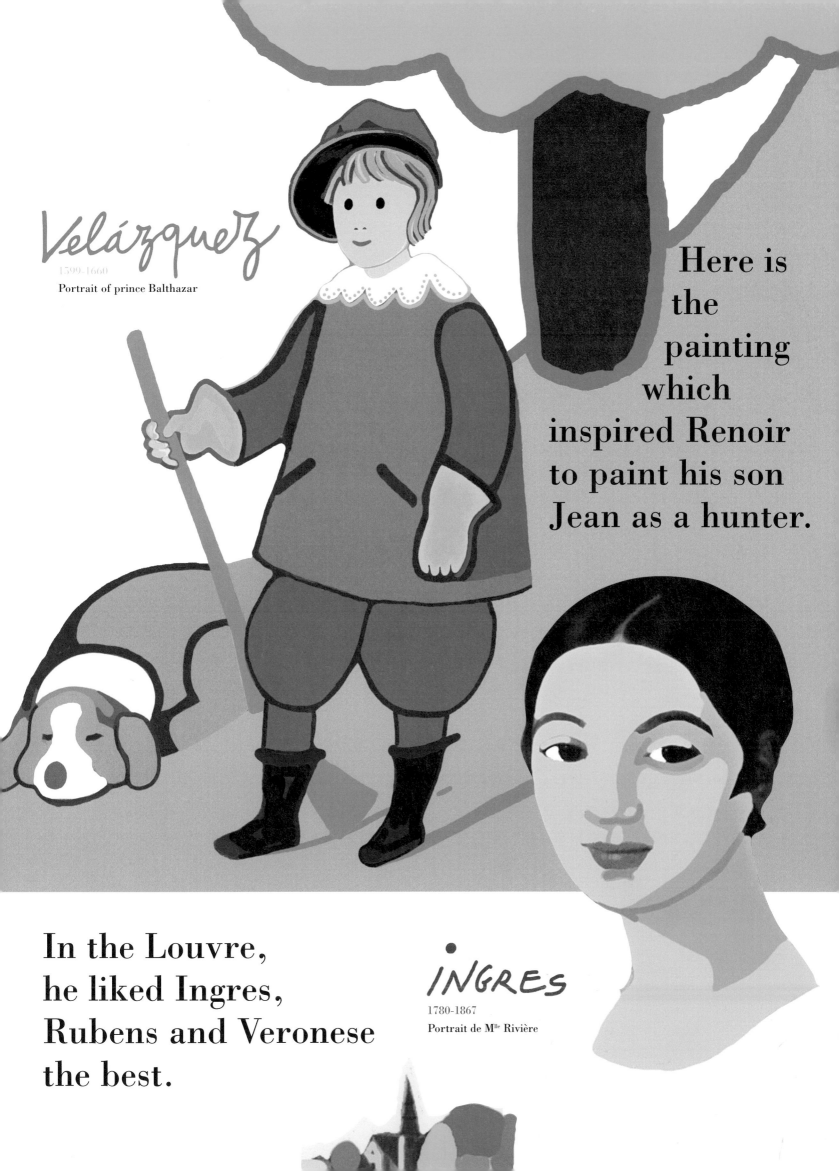

Velázquez
1599-1660
Portrait of prince Balthazar

Here is
the
painting
which
inspired Renoir
to paint his son
Jean as a hunter.

In the Louvre,
he liked Ingres,
Rubens and Veronese
the best.

INGRES
1780-1867
Portrait de Mlle Rivière

Have you noticed the natural style and simplicity of Renoir's paintings?

If you draw horizontal, vertical and diagonal lines, you see immediately that the subjects are naturally positioned in the middle of the painting, surrounded by calm and harmonious compositions.

A glance is enough to understand Renoir's intention.

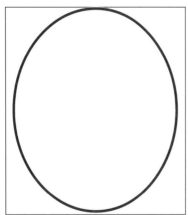

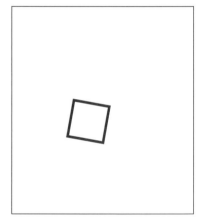

The oval form holds them together.

The shaded square brings depth and volume to the painting.

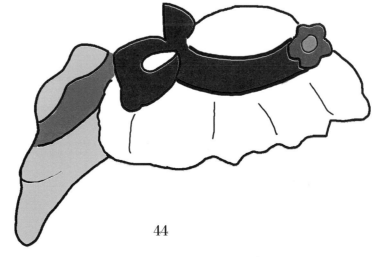

With this painting, you can clearly see that everything is logically positioned. Look closely at the young girl who is standing and leaning forward. Look at her open arms – see how they draw your eye to the centre of the canvas, and create a wonderful sense of protection. Can you see, also, the oval which is formed by the hands moving in tune with the music, as if they were dancing a ballet?!

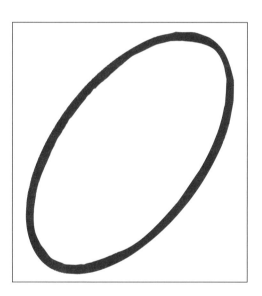

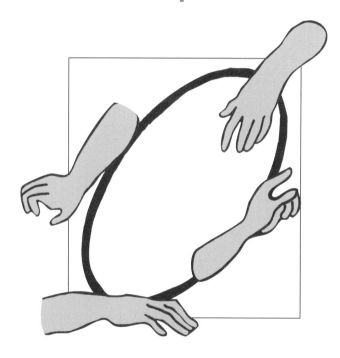

Renoir made several different versions of this painting but if you look closely, you'll notice in the corners that the curtains always go diagonally from the top, and that at the bottom you'll find a music score, or a hat, which makes your eye follow this diagonal line.

Have fun and look for the balance in these compositions.

LOOK!

How many hats can you find in all these paintings by Renoir?

AND YOU TOO

So that you remember everything you see, always carry a notebook and pencil in your pocket, like an artist.
You will then be able to make sketches of all the paintings you like.

Note the colors and the artist's name.

Raphael

Important dates, name of the museum, draw a detail......

Even if you just scribble, you will remember it forever!

PAINTINGS IN THIS BOOK

Pierre Auguste Renoir
Deux jeunes filles lisant,
1891, Los Angeles,
Los Angeles County
Museum of Art

Pierre Auguste Renoir
Jeune fille à la gerbe,
1888, Sao Paulo,
Museu de Arte

Pierre Auguste Renoir
Le Déjeuner des canotiers,
1881, Washington,
Philips Collection

Pierre Auguste Renoir
*Bal du Moulin
de la Galette,* 1876,
Paris, musée d'Orsay

Pierre Auguste Renoir
La Balançoire,
1876, Paris,
musée d'Orsay

Pierre Auguste Renoir
Paysage à Beaulieu,
c. 1893, San Francisco,
Fine Arts Museum,
Mildred Anna Williams
Collection

Pierre Auguste Renoir
La Seine à Argenteuil,
1874, Oregon, Portland
Art Museum

Claude Monet
Régates à Argenteuil,
c. 1872, Paris,
musée d'Orsay

Pierre Auguste Renoir
*Portrait de Madame
Charpentier et ses enfants,*
1878, New York,
The Metropolitan
Museum of Art

Pierre Auguste Renoir
Danse à la campagne,
1882, Paris, musée d'Orsay

Pierre Auguste Renoir
Danse à Bougival,
1883, Boston,
Museum of Fine Arts

Pierre Auguste Renoir
Danse à la ville,
1882, Paris,
musée d'Orsay

Pablo Picasso
La Danse villageoise,
1922, Paris, musée Picasso

Pierre Auguste Renoir
Gabrielle et Jean,
1895, Paris,
musée de l'Orangerie

Pierre Auguste Renoir
Claude Renoir jouant,
1905, Paris,
musée de l'Orangerie

Pierre Auguste Renoir
*Portrait de Claude Renoir.
Coco à la charlotte,*
1902, private collection

Pierre Auguste Renoir
Le Pierrot blanc,
1901, Detroit, The Detroit
Institute of Arts, gift of
Robert H. Tannahill

Pierre Auguste Renoir
Claude Renoir en clown,
1909, Paris,
musée de l'Orangerie

Pablo Picasso
Paul en Pierrot,
1925, Paris, musée Picasso

Pierre Auguste Renoir
Jean Renoir dessinant,
1901, Richmond,
The Virginia Museum
of Fine Art

Pierre Auguste Renoir
Jean Renoir en chasseur,
1910, Los Angeles,
Los Angeles County
Museum of Art, gift of Jean
Renoir and Dido Renoir

Diego Velázquez
*Portrait du prince
Balthazar Carlos
en costume de chasse,*
c. 1635, Madrid,
Museo del Prado

Pierre Auguste Renoir
*Jeunes filles regardant
un album,*
1892, Richmond,
Virginia Museum
of Fine Arts,
The Adolph D. and Wilkins
C. Williams Fund

Pierre Auguste Renoir
*Berthe Morisot et sa fille,
Julie Manet,* 1894, Paris,
private collection

Pierre Auguste Renoir
Jeunes filles au piano,
1892, Paris
musée d'Orsay

Pierre Auguste Renoir
*Jeune femme cousant
à la fenêtre,* 1908-1910,
New Orleans,
Museum of Art,
gift of Ch. C. Henderson
in memory of
M. Henderson

Pierre Auguste Renoir
Gabrielle reprisant,
1908,
private collection

Pierre Auguste Renoir
Gabrielle lisant,
1906, Karlsruhe, Staatliche
Kunsthalle Karlsruhe

Pierre Auguste Renoir
*La Toilette,
Femme se peignant,*
1908, Paris, musée d'Orsay

Pierre Auguste Renoir
Gabrielle à la rose,
1911, Paris,
musée d'Orsay

Pierre Auguste Renoir
Les Vignes à Cagnes,
1908, Brooklyn,
The Brooklyn Museum of
Arts, gift of Colonel and
Mrs. F. W. Garbisch

Pierre Auguste Renoir
La Ferme des Collettes,
1915, Cagnes-sur-Mer,
musée Renoir

Pierre Auguste Renoir
*Terrasses
à Cagnes-sur-Mer,*
1905, Tokyo,
Bridgestone Museum of Art

Paul Cézanne
*La Montagne
Sainte-Victoire,*
1885-1895, Merion,
The Barnes Foundation

Pierre Auguste Renoir
*La Montagne
Sainte-Victoire,*
c. 1888-1889,
New Haven, Yale University
Art Gallery

Pierre Bonnard
Coup de soleil,
1923, Madrid,
Collection Carmen
Thyssen-Bornemisza,
on loan from the Museo
Thyssen-Bornemisza

Pierre Auguste Renoir
*Baigneuse
aux cheveux longs,*
c. 1895, Paris,
musée de l'Orangerie

Pierre Auguste Renoir
Baigneuse,
1892,
private collection

Pierre Auguste Renoir
*Baigneuse assise dans
un paysage*, dite *Eurydice,*
1895, Paris,
musée Picasso

Pierre Auguste Renoir
Baigneuse,
1903, Vienna
Osterreiche Galerie

Pablo Picasso
Nu assis s'essuyant le pied,
1921, Berlin,
Staatliche Museen,
Nationalgalerie,
Museum Berggruen

Pablo Picasso
Grande baigneuse,
1921, Paris,
musée de l'Orangerie

Pierre Auguste Renoir
Les Laveuses de Cagnes,
c. 1912,
private collection

Pierre Auguste Renoir
*Les Laveuses
à Cagnes-sur-Mer,*
c. 1912,
private collection

Pierre Auguste Renoir
*Portrait
de Paul Durand-Ruel,*
1910, private collection

Pierre Auguste Renoir
*Portrait
d'Ambroise Vollard,
en costume de toréador,*
1917, Tokyo,
Nippon Television Network
Corporation (Shibayama)

Pierre Auguste Renoir
*Autoportrait
de l'artiste avec
son chapeau blanc,*
1910, private collection

First published in French 2009 by
Réunion des musées nationaux, Paris

This English-language edition published 2010 by
A&C Black Publishers
36 Soho Square
London W1D 3QY
www.acblack.com

© 2009 RMN

ISBN : 978-1-4081-2384-3

Mila Boutan has asserted her rights under the Copyright,
Design and Patents Act, 1988, to be identified as the Author
of this work.

Translated from the French by Sasha Wardell

Printed in Belgium

REPRODUCTION COPYRIGHTS

BERLIN : Staatliche Museen, Nationalgalerie, Museum Berggruen © BPK, Berlin, Dist
Rmn/Jenz Ziehe, p. 35
BOSTON : Museum of Fine Arts © Giraudon/The Bridgeman Art Library, p. 13
CAGNES-SUR-MER : Musée Renoir © Giraudon/The Bridgeman Art Library, p. 31
DETROIT : The Detroit Institute of Arts, p. 19
KARLSRUHE : Staatliche Kunsthalle Karlsruhe, © Akg-images, p. 28
LOS ANGELES : Los Angeles County Museum of Art © Josse/Leemage, p. 23, 24
MADRID : On loan from Museo Thyssen-Bornemisza, collection Carmen Thyssen-Bornemisza,
p. 33 • Museo del Prado © Akg-images /Erich Lessing, p. 23
MERION : The Barnes Foundation © Giraudon /The Bridgeman Art Library, p. 32
NEW HAVEN : Yale University Art Gallery/Art Resource © Scala Archives, Florence, p. 32
NEW YORK : Brooklyn Museum of Art: Gift of Colonel and Mrs. E.W. Garbisch © Giraudon
/The Bridgeman Art Library, p. 30
The Metropolitan Museum of Art © Metropolitan Museum of Art, Dist. Rmn, p. 10, 11 (details)
NEW ORLEANS : Museum of Art: gift of Charles C. Henderson in memory of Margaret
Henderson, p. 28
PARIS : Réunion des musées nationaux : © J.-G. Berizzi, p. 13, 21 – © H. Lewandowski, p. 4,
5, 6, 9, 12, 13, 14, 16, 27, 28, 29 – © R.-G. Ojéda, p. 34 – © F. Raux, p. 17, 20, 34, 35
PORTLAND : Portland Art Museum © Giraudon/The Bridgeman Art Library, p. 8
RICHMOND : The Virginia Museum of Fine Arts, p. 22, 25
SAN FRANCISCO : Fine Arts Museum © Giraudon/The Bridgeman Art Library, p. 7
SAO PAULO : Museu de Arte © Giraudon/The Bridgeman Art Library, p. 3
TOKYO : Bridgestone Museum of Art © Akg-images/Erich Lessing, p. 31 • Nippon Television

Network Corporation (Shibayama), p. 38
VIENNA : Osterreiche Galerie © Luisa Ricciarini /Leemage, p. 34
WASHINGTON : Collection Philips © Akg-images, p. 4, 6
COLLECTIONS PARTICULIÈRES : p. 18, 28, 38, 39 © Akg-images - p. 25 © Christie's Images -
p. 34 © Giraudon/The Bridgeman Art Library/Peter Willi

Front cover – 1st row l. to r.: Pierre Auguste Renoir, *Jeune fille à la gerbe*, 1988, Sao Paulo,
Museu Arte © Giraudon/The Bridgeman Art Library; Pierre Auguste Renoir, *Le Pierrot
blanc*, 1901, Detroit, The Detroit Institute of Arts, gift of Robert H. Tannahill; Pierre
Auguste Renoir, *Gabrielle et Jean*, 1895, Paris, musée de l'Orangerie, Réunion des musées
nationaux © H. Lewandowski.
2nd row l. to r.: Pierre Auguste Renoir, *Portrait de Claude Renoir. Coco à la charlotte*, 1902,
private collection © Akg-images; Pierre Auguste Renoir, *Jeunes filles au piano*, 1892, Paris,
musée d'Orsay, Réunion des musées nationaux © H. Lewandowski; Pierre Auguste Renoir,
Claude Renoir en clown, 1909, Paris, musée de l'Orangerie, Réunion des musées nationaux ©
F. Raux.
3rd row, l. to r.: Pierre Auguste Renoir, *Le déjeuner des canotiers*, 1881, Washington,
collection Philipps © Akg-images; Pierre Auguste Renoir, *Paysage à Beaulieu*, c. 1893, San
Francisco, Fines Arts Museum, Mildred Anna Williams Collection © Giraudon/The
Bridgeman Art Library; Pierre Auguste Renoir, *Bal du Moulin de la Galette*, 1876, Paris,
musée d'Orsay, Réunion des musées nationaux © H. Lewandowski.
Back cover: Pierre Auguste Renoir, *Le Pierrot blanc*, 1901, Detroit, The Detroit Institute of
Arts, gift of Robert H. Tannahill
All Rights Reserved.

Head of book publishing department
Catherine Marquet

Editor
Josette Grandazzi

Photographic researchers
Consuelo Crulci
Frédérique Kartouby

Production
Hugues Charreyron

Graphic Design
Catherine Collette

Photo-engraving
IGS, L'Isle d'Espagnac

Printed and bound in Belgium
Deckers-Snoeck (Antwerp)

According to Law no.49 956 on the 16 July 1949 for
childrens publications.